P9-DMZ-094

This book is presented to

_____

It was given to you by

_____

Date

_____

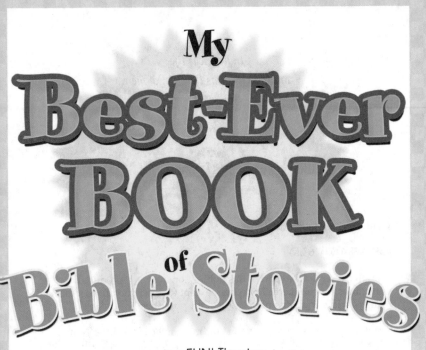

# My Best-Ever BOOK of Bible Stories

Bible Stories! Rhyming FUN! Timeless truth for everyone!

## Phil A. Smouse

### BARBOUR BOOKS
An Imprint of Barbour Publishing, Inc.

*In him was life,*
*and that life was the light of men.*
JOHN 1:4 NIV

© 2011 by Phil A. Smouse

ISBN 978-1-62416-253-4

Scripture quotations marked NIV are taken from the HOLY BIBLE, NEW INTERNATIONAL VERSION®. NIV®. Copyright © 1973, 1978, 1984, 2010 by Biblica, Inc.™ Used by permission. All rights reserved worldwide.

Published by Barbour Books, an imprint of Barbour Publishing, Inc., P.O. Box 719, Uhrichsville, Ohio 44683, www.barbourbooks.com

*Our mission is to publish and distribute inspirational products offering exceptional value and biblical encouragement to the masses.*

Member of the
Evangelical Christian
Publishers Association

Printed in the United States of America.

05012 0315 UG

# Contents

# The Creation Story

In the beginning, way back at its birth,
God created the heavens and cooked up the earth.
Without a big-bang or a pop or a fizz—
out of *nothing at all*—He made all that there is!

The earth was asleep in the darkness of night—
until God told the darkness, "Now let there be light!"
*And light was!* And that very first blazing, clear light
was the light of His glory, His love, and His might.

God looked at the light. He saw it was good.
It was lighting things up just the way that it should.
His love rolled up the darkness and chased it away. . .

There was evening and morning, the very first day.

Then God said, "Let the waters that cover the world
be untangled, uncorked, opened up, and unfurled.
Let them gather above. Let them billow and puff
into cloudy-white, pillowy cotton and fluff.

Let them gather below—let them bubble and splash—
let them babble and gurgle and splatter and crash!

Let the sky stay up high. Let the sea stay down low."
And that's just what they did, as you probably know.
And as *you* may have guessed—and as I now know, too. . .

There was evening and morning on day number two.

Oh, but day number three—it was something to see—
it was something to see back on day number three!
For on day number three God said, *"Now* let there be
lumpy clods of dry sod where there used to be sea!"

And so up from the gurgling, bubbling deep—
up and up from their slumbery, salty, blue sleep,
there arose mighty mountains of muddy, brown goop—
sopping, soggy, wet piles of primordial soup!

God called that goop "land" and the rest he called "sea,"
and He dried it all up just for you and for me.
Then He said, "Let My land produce veggies and fruits,
from their stems and their shoots all the way to their roots!"

So that's just what they did. It was something to see,
on that morning and evening of day number three.

You say your head's spinning? Well, mine's spinning, too.
With all that God's done, what more could He do?
Oh but then, once again, as the night softly spread,
God unfolded the silence and silently said,

"Now let there be lights in the darkness of space—
tiny, twinkling star-lights all over the place—
glassy, golden-light, spinning-white, sparkling spheres.

Let them sing out the seasons and mark out the years!"

And the sun came alive with the gift of His light,
and it shone with the light of His love and His life!
And then high in the inky-blue black of the night
He ker-plopped down the moon to reflect back its light.

What a day? *I should say!* Could there be any more,
after morning and evening on day number four?

But on day number five the whole world came alive—
came alive and went right into wild overdrive!

"Let the waters be filled up with whales and with fish,
and all manner of things that swim, swiggle, and swish.
And then," said the Lord, "let each salmon and tuna
in every last lake, river, sea, and lagoona—

Each grunion and grunt, every grouper and crappie—
each wahoo and halibut mammy and pappy
live happily, *snappily*, every last one
with a million fish daughters and little fish sons!

Let the skies fill with twittering, chirping, and tweeting,
with cock-a-doo doodling, honking, and peeping—
with chickadees, hummingbirds, roosters, and hens—
tufted titmouses, red robins, and wrens!

God saw all the dancing and splashing and singing,
the laughter and joy that His love had been bringing.
He saw it was good. It was free and alive!

There was morning and evening on day number five.

Then on day number six God pulled ALL the stops.
Of all days—some say—that *this day* was tops!
For when *this day* was through, all that God had begun—
all the work that He worked—would at last be all done.

"Let the land dart and scurry with fuzzy and furry things—
*wild and wonderful,* cuddly and purry things!
Lions and tigers and zebras and yaks,
topped with horns and antennas—with antlers and racks.

Hairy things. *Scary things!* Up-all-nightmarey things!
Cute little, snuggle-me-soft, teddy-beary things.
Doo-dads and whatzits and thingamajigs.
Porcupines—prairie dogs—pot-bellied pigs!

Let them toddle and flip. Let them slither and sprawl.
Let the land creep and crawl with new life, big and small!"

God looked all around and He saw it was good.
Every thing did its thing just the way that it should.
Every happy new heart sang His praise, loud and clear,
for they knew something BIG was about to appear.

"Now let Us make man—let Us make him alone—
in Our image and likeness," said God from His throne.
Let him love and be loved. Let him know and be known.
Let him rule Our creation and make it his home."

So in His own image God made up the man—
male and female He made them, just as He'd planned.
Without cavemen or monkeys or riddles or tricks. . .

There was evening and morning on day number six.

On day seven God rested from all He had done.
He had finished the work that His hands had begun.
And he took that one day, and He called that day blessed,
and He set it apart there from all of the rest.

So this Sunday, I think I know just what I'll do:
I'll plop down on my knees and say, "Thanks!"
Wouldn't you?

For each breath that we take—every beat of our hearts—
is a *gift*, and without Him we truly would not
have one slender, slim thing. *We'd have nothing.* It's true!

Oh the depth of His love! *I'll remember.* Will YOU?

# Adam and Eve

Genesis 2:4–3:24

By the sound of His voice, in the still of the night,
long before the first whisper of darkness or light,
on a wee-tiny, shiny, blue ball out in space
God began an amazing, mysterious place.

For with hands never heard, and with eyes never seen
God created a garden—silent and green—
then filled it with things that hum, bubble, and buzz—
full of all that there is, ever *would be*, or was!

But something was missing—some one or some *who*.
So God reached down in to the muck and the goo,
and there, with a handful of soggy, wet sod,
from a squishy-wet, wee, water-loggy, brown clod,

from the dust and the dirt—from the muck and the clay—
God created the very first man on that day!

And that man who God made from the dust and debris,
yes that made-out-of-muddy-brown-muck-man is ME!

And God breathed and said, *"Adam"*—and POW! I arose.
Then He washed off my hands and untangled my toes
and said, *"Pick up your clippers and haul out the hose—*
*go take care of My garden and see that it grows!"*

So I watered the lilies. I fluffed up the flowers.
I patted the bunnies for hours and hours.

But oh, I was lonely as lonely can be.
Not one bunny or bee was as lonely as me!
For as often I say, and as everyone knows,
every guy needs a girl everywhere that he goes.

So one night as I snuggled all soft in my bed—
as sweet visions and dreams danced around in my head—
God knelt down and He plucked-out a rib from my side. . .

*And He made me my very own beautiful bride!*

Well I looked at that girl and my heart went KER-THUMP!
My poor throat crimped and crinkled-up into a lump!
But I reached out my hand—*and she reached out hers, too!*
It was love at first how-do-you, *wow*-do-you do!

And right there in the night we embraced—and we kissed.
Then we both heard God's voice. . .

We both heard Him say this:

"I Am God. I Am One. I Am Faithful and True!
I made all of this stuff just for you and for you.
You may fill up your tummies with gladness and glee
with the yummy, good fruit found on any old tree.

But whatever you hear and whatever you do,
you must never—not ever—chomp, nibble, or chew
on the juicy, pink fruit of THIS tree—not at all.

If you eat from this tree, if you dare to, or try,
on the day that you do you will both surely die!"

So we did what God said. Yes, we did what we should,
because God was our God, and oh boy, was God good!
We'd both giggle and play every night and each day. . .

till we met up with old you-know-who, as they say!

He thlid-down from that tree with a thlippery thlump,
then he curled up his rump in a leathery lump,
and he slithered right up to my sweet, little wife
and with four little words, that snake ruined our life!

*"Did God really say?"* hissed that slobbery slug,
"You must never gulp, nibble, chomp, gobble, or glug
from the yummy, pink fruit found on every good tree
in my beautiful garden of Eden—*did He?"*

"It's a joke. It's a trick. It's a fib and a lie!
Go ahead—eat the fruit. *You will not surely die!"*

Eve looked at the fruit, and you know, it looked good!
And for one tiny second she thought that she could
just go right on ahead and just do her own thing—

as if God wasn't there. As if God didn't care—
as if God wasn't God every day, everywhere!

So she did it! She ate it!
Then I ate it, too!

And the very next half-a-split-second we knew. . .

I looked up at Eve, and then Eve looked at me. . .
Then Eve started to *scream*, and I started to flee!
For I noticed her toe—then she noticed my knee.
So she jumped in a bush, and I ran up a tree!

And *right then and right there,* as we quivered and quaked,
we both knew we'd been tricked by that sneaky old snake.

But we did what we did, and we *knew* we were wrong—
*and we knew that God knew*—so it wouldn't be long
till we'd both have to face Him, and face Him we would.
And we knew He'd remove us from Eden for good.

And that's just what God did.
*But we gave Him no choice.*
Our hearts were both fooled
by that sneaky snake's voice!

The devil's a **LIAR.**
*He always will be!*

So whatever you hear, and whatever you do,
and *whatever* that snake tries to get you to do,
please remember God's love—and remember our sin.
There is only one God. Listen only to Him!

# Daniel and the LION'S DEN

Daniel 6

Well, hello there again. Getting ready for bed?
Oh, you'd like to hear one more quick story instead?
Then hold on to your bear or your beanie-bag buddy,
get comfy and snug and we'll sit back and study

the tale of a godly, good government guy—
a government guy who would not cheat or lie!
No really! It's true! Yes, he did and he was!
I'm not making it up. And I wouldn't because

God expects *truth*. And so Daniel was true—
Just as true as true-blue ever did or could do!

Daniel did his job well. In fact HE was the best.
He was honest and truthful, wise, thoughtful, and blessed.
So you'd think that his work-mates would *love* him—they must!
But they HATED his godly, good, governing guts.

So those grouchy old guys took their grumpy gray heads
and they thought up a plan to *destroy* Dan instead—
they'd catch him red-handed, smack dab in the act
of some low down-and-dirty misdeed, but in fact,

though they slinked and they spied and they privately-eyed
every deed Daniel did and each thing that he tried,
all those grumpy old goobers could not find one tad,
or wee, slender, small thing Daniel did that was bad!

Yes, those grouchy old guys were confused and perplexed.
They were scratching their heads over what to do next.
When right-up and on-out of their angry, numb noodles
came thoughts so pitch-blackened by oodles and oodles

of years lived outside of the goodness of God,
that they pestered and festered and nibbled and gnawed
at the place *in their hearts* that was faithful and true,
and just chewed a big hole right-on-out and clean through!

"If he *will not* do something that's creepy and stinky,
we'll make something up!" they all said, "so I think we
should wind-up our wits and think-up a new plan
to get rid of that godly, good government man."

So the very next day they marched up to the king,
and they smiled a big smile as they started to spring
their deceitful, dishonest, despicable trick.
But the king never knew. It was over that quick!

"O great king!" they sang out, all whipped-creamy and sweet,
"We bow down and we kiss your two hairy, brown feet!
For your humble, wise servants do wish and agree
that the king should proclaim a new royal decree,

that whoever would dare to give worship or praise,
or to kneel down and pray for the next thirty days,
unto anyone other than your own sweet self
should be rounded on up from each closet and shelf,

and then thrown to the lions—both damsel and dude—
to be chomped on and chewed like a sack of fast food!"

"Well, that sounds good to me! Yes, that sounds like great fun.
So let's let it be written and let it be done!"
And with that the king signed a new royal decree,
that could NEVER be changed—not one "Q" or one "T."

Not by king or by queen.
Not by damsel or dude.
Not till thirty long,
nail-chomping days
would conclude!

*Law of the Medes and Persians*
*J. Darius.....*

Well, when Daniel found out, it was truly a shock.
Oh, but what did he do? Did he shudder and knock?
Did he run for the hills? Did he whimper and bend?
Did he crawl in a hole and just try to pretend

that he *was not* a mighty, young man after God?
He DID NOT! For like you, he was caught up and awed
by the wonder and love of his HEAVENLY King.
And so Daniel did not change one wee little thing.

He went up to his room and tore open the shutters,
and prayed till the walls and the roof and the gutters
all shook with the furious, wild, love of God—
till his heart and his mind and his chubby, wee bod

were alive with new life. Yes, he prayed and he prayed,
which is just what he did at that time *every* day!

So they rounded him up like they said that they would.
Oh, those grumpy old guys thought they had him, but good!
For the king had no choice! He would have to conclude,
Daniel broke his new law and would have to be chewed.

Yes, the king knew that Daniel was faithful and true—
he was true as true-blue ever did or could do!
But he made that dumb law, and he knew he'd been tricked.
And quite soon little Daniel'd be lapped up and licked

by those hungry, young lions—those fangs and those claws!
Oh, but what could he do? Not one thing! So he paused,

and said, "Throw him on in—he would not hide his faith—
*but may God whom he serves keep him comfy and safe!*"
Then the king ran away to his kingly sized bed,
and poor Daniel was thrown in and left there for dead!

And deep down in that hole, with those big, hungry guys,
what wee Daniel DID do should have been no surprise.
For as often I say, and as everyone knows,
every cat loves to pray everywhere that he goes!

So they pulled up their rocks and their chairs and their pews
and they said their hellos and their how-do-you-dos.
Then they passed the whole night—the whole godly, good time—
in Isaiah eleven, verse six through verse nine!

But the king couldn't sleep. He was up the whole night,
just a' tossing and turning the way that you might
if your very best friend was alone in the zoo
all because of a dippy-thing done just by *you!*

So he ran to the den and tore open the door,
and yelled, "Dan, are you down there?"
Dan yelled back, "Oh sure!
We were just going to close with a quick word of prayer,
and then once we clean up, I'll be out and right there!"

Now as you surely know, having church the whole night
can *work up* a powerfully strong appetite.
So when Daniel walked out, guess who got thrown in. . .

We'll just leave it at that.
Liars never do win.

# DaVid and Goliath

"BIGGER is better. Yes, bigger is *best*.
When you're BIGGER you're better than all of the rest.
For as everyone knows, and can gladly recall,
when you're dinky and small you don't matter at all!"

Is THAT what you're thinking? Is that what you said?
Is that what's been running around in your head?

Well, just settle-on-down in your chair or your bed
with your mom or your dad or your great-uncle Ted
and I think, if you listen, you're going to see
that BIG isn't all that it's cracked up to be!

BIGGER IS BETTER!

Two armies were gathered on two distant hills.
But the army on one gave the other the chills!
Both armies were fuming and ready to fight,
and it looked like at any time now they just might—

when what to their wondering eyes did appear,
but a creature so terrible, mean, and severe
that each man in *God's* army—each soldier and spear—
was french-frazzled with fear from the front to the rear!

He was biggeth and talleth and largeth and higheth.
He stretched from the ground straight up to the sky-eth!
Armed to the teeth both above and beneath;
a big, burly, Philistine *giant*—

Goliath!

But *this* was no jolly-green "ho-ho-ho" boy.
No, THIS was a NINE-FOOT-TALL search-and-destroy-boy—
a steaming mad, armor-clad, Oscar-the-Grouch,
with a burning desire to make you say, *"Ouch!"*

"YOO-HOO? Boys!" Goliath spat.
"Come out and play—I brought my bat!
You say you're all fuming and ready to fight?
Then *put up your dukes!* Have at it—all right?"

So they put up their dukes—every one, one and all—
but their dukes were all saggy and baggy and small,
and they knew if they made just one pip or wee-squeak,
he would round them and pound them clean into next week!

"Okay, I'm a reasonable, sensitive guy,
and I see," said Goliath, "you're ready to cry.
So I'll make you a deal. Yes, here's just what I'll do.
Here's a special one-time-only offer for you:

I'll fight for *my* army—just little old me—
against one of *your* men. So then, who will it be?
Yes, that will be lovely! Oh, that *will* be fun,
and there won't be a mess to clean up when we're done!"

"Come on, what's the matter?" he bellowed and thundered.
"Please step right on up and get clobbered and plundered!
Don't want to get dirty? Still frozen with fright?
*Well then maybe your MOMMIES will come out and fight!*"

So, night after night after day after day,
on and on went Goliath that very same way.
And for forty long days, on their side of the hill,
they just stood there like statues, and took it, until. . .

A wee-tiny fellow, so dinky and small
that you'd hardly believe he would matter at all,
wandered into the camp and just happened to hear
all the, *"fee-fie-foe-fum!"* that had filled them with fear.

"Just who does this Philistine think that he is?"
said that dinky, small dude with that big voice of his.
"He's insulting the army of Almighty God!
but he'll do it *no more,* over my own wee-bod!"

Well now, THAT kind of talk turned some heads right away.
No, that's not like the thing that you hear every day!

So when word got around, that wee-dinky, small dude
was shipped off to the king, who was coming unglued.
Yes, the king was *upset*. And why shouldn't he be?
He had to whip someone as big as a TREE!

Oh, but when he saw David, his tummy flip-flopped.
His heart sunk down to his sandals and stopped.
They needed a hero—a fighting *machine*.
But Dave looked like HE couldn't whip a sardine!

"This kid is a tadpole! A pee-wee! A guppy!
We need a HE-MAN," said the king, "not a *puppy*.
Now, pardon me, son. You're a cute little tyke,
*but we need a KING KONG—not a boy on a bike!*"

"My name, sir, is *David*, and if I may say,"
said that wee-tiny guy in his extra-large way,
"that I've beat up a bear and I've clobbered a lion,
and whipped them both *good*, sir—without even tryin'!

For GOD is my strength, and although I'm quite small,
by His might and His power *Goliath will fall!*
You say you need someone who's manly and tough?
Then come over here king, and I'll show you my stuff!"

"Well, aren't *you* a spunky, young, godly, good guy!
All right," said the king, "let's go give it a try."

So the king gave wee David his helmet and boots,
and his shield and his sword and his giant-proof suit,
and he figured that David was ready to fight,
when in fact he was locked-down and frozen-up tight!

"I CAN'T fight like this! Man, I can't even see!
This might work for YOU, but it won't work for ME.
I said this before, but I'll say it again:
*It's GOD who will fight, and it's GOD who will win!"*

So David de-booted, disrobed, and undressed.
He untangled that old tin-can-tankerous mess,
bolted down to the stream, gathered five smooth, small stones,
then took off like the wind, bent to rattle some bones!

"*Hey, giant!*" Dave yelled.
"Yeah, I'm talking to YOU!
Hey, I'm telling you just what I'm going to do!
You've insulted the army of Almighty God—
Now you better get ready to swallow some sod!"

Well, Goliath looked down just below his left knee,
oh, and what, to his wondering eyes, did he see
but a wee-teeny fellow, so dinky and small
that you'd hardly believe he could matter at all!

"*What am I, A DOG?!?*" thundered mean old Goliath,
"that you send me this wee-teeny, not-very-higheth,
pink, peach-fuzzy pup with a stick and some rocks?
Oooh, I'm shakin' the whole way on down to my socks."

*"Well then fight like a man!"* rumbled dinky, small Dave.
"What's the matter, you sissy? Come on—*make my day!*
This battle is GOD'S, and in GOD'S mighty name,
on this day *I'M the hunter* and YOU are the GAME!"

And so out came his sling, and then in went a stone,
and wee, dinky, small Dave, in a way all his own,
slung it 'round and around and around and about,
and that one tiny, smooth-shiny pebble flew out. . .

like a photon-torpedo—like *lightning* it sped—
and it bopped old Goliath right-square in the head!

"My word!" said Goliath, "You ARE a good shot!
I was going to duck, but I guess I forgot.
Why is everyone spinning? Who turned out the lights?
Is it nap time already? Oh well, nighty-night!"

And right there in that spot,
in the blink of an eye,
that gigantic, enormous,
big muscle-bound guy
went as soft as a Twinkie—
he pitched and he yawed. . .

And fell down with a

**CRASH!**

fat-head-first in the sod.

You can puff yourself up. It won't help you at all.
For the bigger you are, then the harder you'll fall.
But when GOD is your strength, you're a hundred feet tall. . .

Even though you're the smallest, wee person of all.

# The Fiery Furnace

SOME KINGS ARE OKAY.

Some kings are okay. And some kings are all right.
And some kings do *some things* better kept out of sight.
Oh, but now and again, though you pray—and you *must*—
you wind up with a king who's just chock-full-of-nuts!

Like King Nebuchadnezzar. King Nebooka-who?
*Just the nuttiest king that the world ever knew!*
A king "way-back-when" worse than old "you-know-who"?
Oh yes—even *those* kings were *completely nuts*, too!

For one day as Neb sat on his kingly behind,
as he did his king-thing IT popped into his mind. . .
Just one teeny, small thought. Just a tiny to-do.

But it *grew*

and it grew

and it GREW

and it GREW.

And he thought,
"Well, why not!
I'm the king, am I not?

And besides,
I have nothing much
better to do!"

So he gathered together each nickel and dime—
every bright, golden, twinkling-thing he could find—
every nugget and trinket. Each coin and doubloon,
and he melted and smelted from morning till noon. . .

He fashioned an image.
*An idol.* A LIE!—
nearly nine feet around—
almost ninety feet high!

Well, he looked at that thing, and that thing looked at him,
and that big, fat, king-head of his started to swim!

So he called for his pipe, and he called for his bowl,
and he called for each person he ruled or controlled,
and he lined them all up just as straight as can be,
and pronounced and proclaimed his toot-fruity decree:

"Oh, peoples and nations and men of all tongues!"
yelled king Nebby's yell-boy at the top of his lungs,

"When your ears hear the toots of the fifes and the flutes,
when the choir honks and hoots their kazoos and kazoots,
when the harps start to plink, and the band tweets and twitters,
and patters and pitters their bells and their zithers,

FALL FLAT ON YOUR FACE! For the king does command,
as you crinkle and bake in the burning-hot sand,
as you simmer and sizzle with glee and with pleasure—

*WORSHIP THIS STATUE OF NEBUCHADNEZZAR!"*

So every last person of every belief,
every doctor and lawyer and Indian chief,
fell face-down in the sand at king Nebby's command,
*and they worshipped the idol he made with his hand!*

"And, oh yes, by the way, if you will not obey,
on the day you do not, " said the king, "you will pay!
For I've stoked up my furnace red-hotter than hot,
and that's right where you'll go if you dare to do-NOT!"

So as you may have guessed, and as most people would,
all those folks followed orders and followed them good.
Every ONE, that would be, except three little, wee. . .

Except three little, WEE-little, godly, good guys
with a wee-little, pea-little godly surprise.
Three godly, good guys who said, *"NO. We won't go!"*
Shadrach, Meshach, and Abed-nego!

"Can it BE?" asked the king, "that you're *really* so bold
that you will not bow down to my idol of gold?
Now, let's try this again. It's quite easy. You'll see!
Simply open your mouths and repeat after me. . ."

"When your ears hear the toots of the fifes and the flutes,
when the choir honks and hoots their kazoos and kazoots. . . "

"*FALL FLAT ON YOUR FACE!* Yes, we heard your decree.
Your toot-fruity decree is as dumb as can be!

Do whatever you like. Do whatever you will!
Throw us onto your greasy, black, barbeque grill!
But your burning, red-hotter than hot-as-can-be,
flaming, fiery-red furnace WON'T BURN US! You'll see!

For God is our God. HE IS GOD! And we vow,
if He saves us or not, *WE WILL NOT EVER BOW!*"

Oh, but Neb wasn't kidding. No, Nebby was nuts—
from one end to the other—no if's, and's, or but's!

So he fired up the furnace. He made it red-hot—
seven times as red-hot as it ever had got!
And he opened the door and just threw them right in. . .

But what happened next stopped King Neb in his tracks.
His big tummy flip-flopped. His heart melted like wax!
And his two big bug-eyes popped right out of his head
as he looked in that furnace and quietly said,

"I thought we threw THREE little godly, good men
down there into that fiery, red furnace just then. . .
Oh, but lookie at that. Well now, what do you know?
I see FOUR—and one looks like an ANGEL—OH NO!

Their ropes are untangled. Their clothes are un-burnt!
They're just waltzing and schmaltzing around like they weren't
ever wound-up and bound-up and frittered and fried.

"GET THEM OUT OF THERE NOW!
GET THEM OUT!" the king cried.

So those three walked right out just as cool as you please
as King Nebby fell down on his knobby king knees
and yelled, "Praise be to God! For at last I can see. . . "

"The 'god' that I made, I made all by myself.
Made by money and power—by strength and by wealth.
Throw THAT stuff in the fire and IT would have burned!
Oh, but thanks to you godly, good guys I have learned

that I can not make *God.* Oh, but God *can* make me.
Now my God will *be* God, and His work will be ME!"

# The Walls of Jericho

## You Have Probably Heard. . .

You have probably heard, or may already know,
about Josh and the Great Wall of Jericho—oh!
How we stumbled and stomped all about and around,
and the walls of that town came a' tumblin' down.

But I'll bet my big toe that you never did know,
or may never have heard one mysterious word,
about what happened AFTER
the walls finally fell—

which is what I'm about
both to show *and to tell!*

We were working God's plan. We did just what He said.
Every morning at eight we all jumped out of bed,
and without one wee-peep, sneaker-squeaker, or sound,
we marched up to the city and trotted around,

from one side to the next—through the smog and the haze,
just the way that God said, for six dusty, long days.
For this land was OUR land, and we knew that although
someone put up this city, it all had to GO!

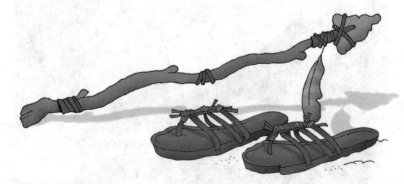

When the seventh day came we all jumped out of bed.
We knew just what to do. *We would do what God said!*
Yes, this city was ours, and it had to ker-plop,
for God said that it would, from the tip to the top.

So we stamped and we stomped and we tramped and we tromped
seven times, all around, till we finally stopped.
Then we filled up our lungs and got ready to shout,
and watch GOD blow those walls straight-on-up and clean out!

"Now remember," I cried, "when the walls tumble down,
we MUST destroy *every last thing* in this town.
Don't pick anything up. Don't take anything home.
Not one toothbrush or Q-tip or greasy, black comb.

For GOD said if we snitch even one little pot,
He will punish us all—so we all better NOT!"

So we blew on our trumpets. We blew them out loud.
Then we started to shout, and the walls tumbled down!
From the east to the west, from the north to the south,
the whole place bit the dust by the words of our mouth!

Oh, but wouldn't you know, in that one certain spot,
there where no one would know if he did or did not—
there where no one would see, could be seen, or get caught,
Achan saw it—and TOOK IT—and knew he should NOT!

For it glittered and twinkled—it sparkled and shined.
Achan wanted it ALL—all he ever could find!
And he thought that he had IT. But in fact, it had HIM!
It ripped open his heart and just stomped right on in,

and it tangled and choked and in-festered the place
where God once made His home—where He poured out His grace.
And what once was so rich became desperate and poor.
But he just didn't care. All he wanted was MORE!

So he stuffed all that stuff up inside of his shirt
and tip-toadled on back to his tent in the dirt,
and he buried that gold and the stuff that he took
way-down-deeply where nobody ever would look!

"So what's the big deal?" you may wonder today.
"Oh, it's just some old *stuff* anyhow, anyway.
No one ever will know. It will never be missed."
But the problem is not with the stuff, it's with this:

When GOD says "Do not" what he means is "DO NOT!"

And because of the ONE thing that Achan DID do,
more than THIRTY men died. Yes, and Achan died, too!
For God said if they took just one pot or one lid,
He would punish them all, so He had to—and DID!

God's rules are God's rules. He is God. I am not.
I will do what God says, because HE is the boss.
I may not understand. That's completely okay.
I don't need to ask *why*. I will simply obey!

# The Story of Jonah

Jonah 1–4

The Lord's word...

The Lord's word to Jonah came quite unexpected:
"Go down to Nineveh. You've been elected.
Tell all the people there, without delay,
the thing that I tell you to tell them today!"

"Nineveh! Goodness! Of all of the places!
Those Ninevites all have the nastiest faces.
They're rude and they're crude and I'd have to conclude
they're an ill-tempered brood of the worst magnitude.

But I guess that I'll do it. It *is* on my way.
Now what is it, Lord,
that You want me to say?"

That Way

Tarshish

"THUS SAYS THE LORD! This is what you should say:
'Listen up, or I may have to ruin your day!

You're mean, and you're nasty and not very nice,
and those are your GOOD points, to be more precise.
For I mean what I say, and I am quite sincere
when I tell you I smell you the whole way up here!'"

"Tell that to them? You must be mistaken!
You certainly can't expect ME to partake in
a dreadful, impossible scheme," Jonah spat,
"like the one You're suggesting—and that, Lord, is that!"

*How awful, how shocking, how horribly harsh-ish!*
he thought as he boarded a boat bound for Tarshish.
And down in the very most bottomest part,
Jonah laid there alone, just himself and his heart.

Jonah laid in that boat, and he thought and he thought,
but he just couldn't do what he knew that he ought.
Now, you can't run away from the Lord. Jonah knew it.
But he was about to find out what occurs when you DO it!

The weather started getting rough.
The tiny ship was tossed. . .
A tempest blew. The crewmen flew!
The thunder boomed. "We're surely doomed!"
they all presumed, "to be consumed here by this holocaust!"

"All hands on deck, all hands on deck!"
the captain shouted out.
"And Jonah, you get up here, too!
Because, if I am not mistaken,
this earthquaking is the making
of the likes of you."

The crew drew straws to figure out just who should be ejected
for causing this calamity to which they'd been subjected.

The shortest straw would tell them who,
and as he had predicted,
the captain watched with no surprise. . .

*as good old Jonah picked it!*

"Okay, okay,
it's all my fault.
Just throw me out.
The storm will stop!"

"You heard the man. Let's throw him in!"
the sailors shouted with a grin.
"Yes, bon voyage and tallyho,
let's pick him up and heave him, HO!"

"Wait a minute. Not so fast,"
the captain shouted, flabber-gassed.
"Let's try again. Let's make the shore.
Now grab your oars and row some more.
*Stroke, stroke, stroke, stroke!*"

But they simply couldn't do it. . .

So they threw him out in-TO it!

And, all at once, the thunder stopped.
The sea grew calm. The sun came out.

What God did Jonah so betray
to cause this startling display
where even wind and waves obey?

Now deeper and deeper he found himself sinking,
which prompted old Jonah to do some rethinking!

"Oh Lord," Jonah cried, "have You left me for dead?
The waves and the waters encircle my head.
Barnacles clutch at my fingers and toes,
and some wet, wiggly thing is attached to my nose!

Oh, there's nothing, I'm sure,
quite so dreadful as this. . .

Except being swallowed alive by a fish!"

"Inside of a fish! Oh, of all of the places!
Of all of the dreadful, disgraceful disgraces!
I'll do what You ask, Lord! I'll do it Your way.
I'll do it right now, right this minute, today."

So that fish spat up Jonah right there on the beach;
and the minute it did it, Jonah started to preach.

"'Forty more days, says the Lord.' It's a fact.
You've got forty short days left to clean up your act.

For you're mean, and you're nasty and not very nice;
And those are your good points, to be more precise.
God means what He says, and I am quite sincere
when I tell you He smells you the whole way up here!"

Now, everyone there from the king straight on down
was convinced that this guy wasn't fooling around.
So they cleaned up their hearts.
Yes, they cleaned up their act.
And they cleaned it up quick, as a matter of fact.

But forty days passed, and then forty-one,
and the Lord didn't do what He said would be done.

"Lord, what's going on here? I look like a goof.
You said You'd destroy them. Now give me some proof!"

"Proof, My friend Jonah? You don't understand.
All of creation is at My command!

And no matter how angry or hurtful or mean,
unfaithful, unworthy, or selfish you've been,
I'll never reject you or turn you away.
For I love you so deeply, I barely can say."

"I'm waiting, just WAITING, to open My hands. . . "

"And that's why I gave them, and YOU,
one more chance."

# The Story of Ruth

Ruth 1-4

"IT CAN'T BE TRUE!"

"It can't be true! I can't go on!
Oh, everything we had is gone."
Naomi wept. Poor Ruthie cried.
*Naomi's precious sons had died!*

And oh, one precious,
priceless son,
Naomi's son,
that very one,
was Ruthie's
*husband.*

Lord above!
Her one-and-only,
one true love.

Now, sometimes when it rains it pours,
and this time it would pour for sure.

For evil people ruled the land
as evil people sometimes can,
and sometimes will and sometimes do,
when you and I allow them to.

From here to there, from there to here,
the food began to disappear!
It filled the people full of fear—
yes, full of fear from ear to ear!

"Orpah! Ruth!" Naomi cried.
"The time has come. We must decide.
We have to leave. We cannot stay.
We cannot stay, not now—no way."

"From north to south, from west to east,
the men are gone. Extinct. Deceased!
Without a man," Naomi said,
"WE'RE ALL ABOUT AS GOOD AS DEAD!"

(Now ladies, things were different then,
so don't get too upset, amen?)

"Just look at me. I'm old and wrinkled,
sagged and bagged and crook'd and crinkled,
crumpled, puckered, nooked, and crannied,
Rip-Van-Winkled, grayed, and grannied!

Oh, there's just no hope in sight
to find another Mister Right,
or even just a Daffy Duck,
an Elmer Fudd, or Mister Yuck!

The time has come! The time is now.
The time has come right now and how!
You must return, you must, I say,
return back home, right now, today."

Naomi prayed
they'd see the light,
and Orpah knew
that she was right.

She packed her bags
without a fight
and left for home
that very night.

But oh, not Ruth.
Not her. No way.
She had a thing
or two to say. . .

"I can't return. I want to stay.
I will NOT go, right now, today!"

"For where you are
is where I'll be.
And when you stay,
you'll stay with me.

And when you die,
I'll die with you.
And THAT is what
I'm going to do.

*Your God will be MY God, and He
will surely care for you and me!"*

Oh, what a thing for Ruth to say.
That kind of thing can make your day,
and make you shout "hip-hip hooray!"

They hugged and kissed, then packed up tight
and left for Bethlehem that night.

"Naomi! Is it really true?
What happened, girl? Just look at you!

Your hair! Your clothes! Your shoes! Your toes!
Your eyes, your ears, your mouth, your nose!
You're looking pale. You're looking thin.
In fact, if we may say again,
you're really looking more akin
to something that the cat dragged in!"

Well, things looked bad, the way things can,
but listen now, God had a plan. . .

"Oh Naomi, please don't cry.
Oh please don't cry. I'll tell you why.

I'll find a farm. I'll be real nice.
I'll ask them once or maybe twice
to take our jugs and jars and sacks
and fill them full
of treats and snacks."

"Yes, crumbs and morsels, flakes and flecks,
leftover kernels, crumbs, and specks.
A black banana! Bagels! Lox!
Some cheese stuck to a pizza box!

I'll beg and plead. I'll sob and bleat! I'll ask them for a tasty treat—

An itsy-bitsy, teeny-weeny, tiny scrap for us to eat!"

So off she went. She did her thing.
She did it never noticing
that someone had been fastening
his bulging eyes on *everything*.

"Who IS that girl out in my field,
and what's she doing?" Boaz squealed.
"Look AT that hair. Look AT those eyes!
Excuse me just one minute, guys,
I've got to go and socialize!"

He shaved his toes. He licked his lips.
He checked his teeth for cracks and chips.
He combed the bugs out of his hair,
yes, Don Juan double-debonair
with *savoir-faire* extraordinaire!

Now don't be quick to judge, amen?
Well, don't think what you're thinking then.
For Boaz was a gentleman.

"Please stay with us. Take what you need.
Take what you need and more, indeed!"

He loaded up all Ruthie's sacks
and jugs and jars with treats and snacks.
Yes, it WAS *true love* at first sight—
a double thumping-heart delight!

She headed home. *Oh, what she'd found!*
Her world was turning upside down.
She ran the whole way back to town
about ten feet above the ground.

"I'm telling you, tonight's the night,"
Naomi grinned, "and if I'm right,
there's only one thing left to do
to get that man to say I DO!"

So do they did. Oh, DID they do. . .

They fluffed and puffed. They crimped and curled.
They powdered, sweet-perfumed, and pearled!
They thanked the Lord. They sang His praise!
They marveled at His wondrous ways!

And off she went into the night
to have and hold her Mister Right—
her Mister Shining-Armored Knight—
her straight-from-heaven-sent delight!

Now, as I'm sure that you supposed
Boaz said, "YES!" when Ruth proposed.
Yes, RUTH proposed. That's what I said.
Just look it up—go right ahead.

They tied the knot and lived to be
quite happy ever-afterly.
And soon God blessed them with a son,
a precious, little baby one.

But wait! This story's far from done.
Because their son, he was the one
who had a son, who had a kid
known as King David. Yes, he did.

And David was the Great, Great, Great,
Great, Great (times three, times one, plus eight),
Great Grand-dad of a man whose wife
you've likely heard of all your life.

A man whose son, to be precise,
was Jesus. No?! YES! Jesus Christ!

Take a second. Think it through.
Oh, what God will go and do!

For God is love and love is kind,
the kindest that you'll ever find,
the kindest that you'll ever see,

that's something else—don't you agree?

"HAVE YOU NOTICED?"

"Have you noticed My servant? He's gentle and kind,
and our hearts are so sweetly, completely entwined.
He's as good as it gets—the cream of the crop.
The pick of the litter. The tip of the top!"

"And why not?" croaked the devil. "He's as rich as a king.
Why, You've never withheld even one little thing."

"Take away all those whistles and hooters and bells
and I'll bet it's a whole different story he tells!"

Well, that night while Job snoozed in his big easy chair,
as he snurgled and snorgled, he got quite a scare.
Three men came a' busting right into the room
and proceeded to fill him with gloom and with doom!

"Remember those hundreds of camels and sheep,
and the thousands of horses and donkeys you keep
in that field where you used to have millions of goats
by the lake where you always kept all of your boats,

and your barns and your pens
and your coops and your stalls?"

"Well, some burglars came and they burgled it ALL!"

"But it doesn't end there 'cause those down-dirty stinkers
made off with your bangles and jingles and twinklers.
They snatched up your doo dads and gizmos and blinkers!"

Poor Job was astounded. Completely dumbfounded!
His stomach glub-gurgled. His heart pumped and pounded.
But oh, don't you know, he got down on his knees.

*He gave thanks to the Lord just as quick as you please!*

"I just hate all that praising. It makes me quite ill!"
spat the devil. "But I can go one better still. . .
I'll give him some uh-oh's and boo-boo's and stings!
Then I'll bet it's a whole different song that he sings!"

So Job became terribly, scare-ably sick.
He wheezled and woozled.
He hacked and up-hicked!

*"What good is your faith? It's a joke. It's a lie!*
Give up!" Job's wife sputtered.
"Just CURSE GOD AND DIE!"

*"Curse God and die? Curse God and die!?*
I can not. I will not!
But, why, oh Lord,
WHY?"

News travels fast. Oh my, yes, that's the truth!
And THIS news traveled straight to three friends from Job's youth
who took off right that minute, posthaste, PDQ
to find out what was up and see what they could do.

"It just isn't fair. No, it doesn't make sense.
This tragic, traumatical turn of events!
Lord, why be created, composed, or contrived
when I'm better not born, brought about, or alived!"

"Oh, give me a break!" Eliphaz blurted out.
"You've sinned a great sin. There can't be any doubt."

"Just look at yourself. You're a mess! You're a wreck!
You've been up to no good, I suppose and suspect.

We KNOW that Job's utterly
wicked and rotten,
but what does GOD think?
That's the thing we've forgotten!

This punishment's awful.
An outrage! A curse!"
"But it could have, and probably
SHOULD have been worse!"

"What wonderful friends. What exquisite advice!
Did you say you were leaving? Yes, that would be nice!"

"I know that I'm righteous. I haven't a doubt.
My spirit is clean both within and throughout.
And although God destroys me and grinds me to dust,
it is Him who I'll honor, abide in, and trust!

I've done nothing wrong. Yes, I KNOW that it's true.
So, tell me, Lord, WHAT IN THE WORLD DID I DO?"

"What did you do? Oh, if we only knew!"

"You must have been lying or cheating or stealing.
Yes, snitching and sneaking and squawking and squealing.
Oh, how could you do it? Oh, what did you do?
Oh, why are we standing here talking to you?!"

"Just who do you think that you're duping and fooling?
*We're full of it, Job*—full of wisdom and schooling.
Go on," Bildad babbled, "rave, rant, and hiss,
but remember, YOU got your own self into THIS!"

"Lord, why do You slay me? What gives You the right?
Has it done any good? Can it be Your delight?

You know that I'm righteous! I'm gentle and kind,
and our hearts are so sweetly, completely entwined.
Oh, why don't You answer? Oh, where is the man
who would bring us together? Send HIM, if You can!"

"Excuse me," said someone from back in the trees.
"Allow me to add my two cents, if you please."

"These things I've been hearing!
These things you've been speaking!
This non-stop, right-up-to-the-eyeballs critiquing.
You speak against God. Boy, you've all got some guts!
What are you guys, crazy? What are you guys, nuts!?"

Well, those words weren't out of his mouth for one minute
when the next thing I knew, we were standing there in it,
inside of a swirling, twist-twirling black cloud
where we all heard GOD'S voice. Very clear. VERY loud!

"Who filled up the oceans? Who turned on the stars?
Who brought forth Orion? The Milky Way? Mars?
Who made every thing do the thing that it does?
Well I'll tell you: I did and I AM and I was!

*Your home is with ME, Job. It isn't down here."*

"When all this is gone, all the why's and the how's,
all the to's and the fro's, all the here's and the now's,
there still will be you, and there still will be Me.
Together. Forever. Be patient. You'll see!"

So the Lord restored all of Job's cattle and goats,
his wife and his family, his friends and his boats.
And he lived to be more than one hundred and ten.
Very old. A bit wrinkled. Quite happy. Amen!

# Cain and Abel

Genesis 4:1–16

A long time ago, in a faraway place,
near a garden that bloomed with God's love and His grace,
lived two men who were different as different could be—
Cain and Abel, the offspring of Adam and Eve.

Cain worked the soil. He dug and he hoed.
He burrowed and furrowed. He mulched and he mowed.
He weeded and feeded the seed he had sown,
till his garden was monstrously, miracle-grown!

Oh, but Abel was different, for Abel liked sheep.
Yes, he loved them so much he saw sheep in his sleep.
And their baahs and their bleats didn't bug him a bit.
He loved every wooly, wee one he could get.

One day as he wandered and waggled and walked
through the grassy, green hills with his fluffy, white flock,
by the quiet, still water he paused and he stopped. . .
and he thought, *Oh my goodness. I almost forgot!*

"Our God is so good, and He's blessed me so much,
with my little, bo-sheepily people and such,
I should bring Him a present—a thank-ewe—a kid!
So that's just what I'll do." And that's just what he did.

But when Cain saw what Abel was able to do
with his tender, kind heart and his loving thank-ewe,
he looked *down* at the ground, and he grumbled and stewed,
and he thought, *I guess I should give God a gift, too.*

So they both brought the very best gift that they could.
Abel gave his with joy. Cain just knew that he should.
And from way up in heaven, God looked *at their hearts*—
for He knew that *Cain's gift* was *no gift* from the start.

"Cain, why are you angry? Why grumble and stew,
when you KNOW," the LORD said, "what I want you to do?
When you do what is right, it's My joy and delight—
but the choice is one-hundred percent up to you."

But Cain would not listen. He just didn't care
about anyone, any-which-way, anywhere.
So he tuned out God's voice, and the minute he did,
sin was waiting to get him—*and get him it did!*

So he hatched up a plan right up there in his head—
a BIG, bug-eyed, nasty, red, rotten plan fed
by *the devil himself*—by his anger and gall—
to get rid of his brother *for once and for all!*

Cain knew what he did. It was there on his hands.
It was there *in his heart*—on the ground—in the sand.

And the ground cried aloud
for the thing Cain had done.

There was nowhere to go. There was nowhere to run.
There was nowhere to hide from the blazing, hot sun,
as the sound of God's voice, and each drop of red blood
thundered, *"Where is your brother, and what have you done!?"*

"I swear I don't know. God, you surely must see!
I would not have done THAT! It could not have been ME!"
Cain lied and he lied, and way, deep down inside
all the love he once had simply gave up and died.

For the rest of his life—to his very last day—
Cain just wandered and squandered his life clean away.
All his beautiful gardens dried up into dust,
in the very same way that they will, and they must,

when a heart grows so blind, and so callous and cold—
so angry and bitter—so crinkled and old—
that it won't even notice the glittering gold
of the true heart of Jesus in every last soul.

# Nebuchadnezzar's crazy dream

Daniel 4

## OH, LORD, WHAT A DREAM. . .

Oh, Lord, what a *dream*—what a *scare*—what a *fright!*
What a white-knuckled, tooth-grinding, *terrible* night!

My taste buds were tingling—my toenails were taut!
My BIG belly button curled up in a knot!
My tongue twitched and twittered then tangled-up tight.
My eyeballs bugged out with each crazy, new sight!

So I called for my psychics and sayers of sooth,
and I asked them to listen and tell me the truth
of this verily, scare-ily, raise-up-your-hair-ily,
dream that I dreamt by myself, solitarily!

"Listen, King Neb, we've been through this before.
Your dreams are so weird, we can never be sure
if you're seeing the future—it could be, instead,
that you're eating too much spicy food before bed!"

"Too much spicy food? Eating right before bed?
What on earth was I thinking up there in my head?
You really are wise. Please forgive me, " I said.
"Go and get me that new kid—*or you guys are dead!*"

So they went and got Daniel. They brought him upstairs.
They sat him in one of the king's favorite chairs.
They turned and bowed down till their heads touched the ground,
then they shot him their *let's-see-you-do-better* stares!

"Oh, great king," Daniel said, "spit it out. Go ahead.
What's this heart-thumping , goose-bumping,
dream that you dread?"

"The dreaded dream fright-mare that's puzzling me
was a dream of a spreading-wide whopper-sized tree!
It was bigger and better than all of the rest.
It stretched halfway to heaven and blocked out the rest!

And the people, ALL people, looked up to the tree.
It took care of them all quite omnipotently!
And not just the people—the animals too—
every bird, bee, bat, cow, cat, and kanga-ma-roo.

And then, just as quick as my dream had begun,
there stood something or some*one* that shined like the sun!
He *reached down* from the heaven—the lights flickered out.
Then that something or *someone*—he started to *shout!*"

"Chop down the tree. Cut it up. Pull it out!
Lop off its branches, stems, twigs, leaves, and sprouts.
Bind up its stump with a chain made of brass.
Surely these things shall ALL come to pass!

For seven long years let him graze with the cows.
Let him slop with the pigs. Let him grunt with the sows.
Let the dew drench his back and the hair on his head.
Let him know that he knows Who it is who has said,
'The kingdoms are MINE—there is no other one.'

So let it be written. So let it be done!"

Poor Daniel said nothing. His eyeballs popped out.
His jaw hit the floor like a forty-pound trout.

His hair shot straight up on the top of his head,
for he knew what God meant—
*and God meant what He said!*

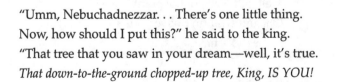

"Umm, Nebuchadnezzar. . . There's one little thing.
Now, how should I put this?" he said to the king.
"That tree that you saw in your dream—well, it's true.
*That down-to-the-ground chopped-up tree, King, IS YOU!*

God wants you to know, Neb, that HE is the Boss,
and *you* and your whopper-sized pride will be tossed
right-on-out of the kingdom, as quick as a flash.
Unless you repent, it's BOOM!—out with the trash!"

Well, old Neb got the point.
Oh, and wouldn't have you?
So he did what God said. . .

For an hour or two.

*"Just look at this place. So majestic. So tall!*
Mighty Nebuchadnezzar—the Lord of it ALL!

My gardens are hanging. My stairways climb high.
My big ziggurats stretch straight up to the sky!
It's all so amazing I hardly can speak.
I'm a big Babylonian right at his peak!

Have I squished a few folks? Sure, but what can I say?
*This kingdom is mine—and I did it my way!"*

And wouldn't you know it—it happened that fast.
All the things Daniel said—*every one* came to pass!

The people arose. They attacked with a shout.
They moved him on-up, and they threw him on-out.
Nebby moo'd with the cows, just the way that God said,
and he did till he finally came to his head.

"Seven long years. Now I finally see.
GOD is the one to be praised—not me!

All those whoopie-ding, I'M-the-king things that I did,
all that look-at-me stuff, oh Lord, heaven forbid
that I ever do any of THAT stuff again.
For You are the King and You always have been!

And not just *a* king, but *the* King of ALL Kings.
The King of all kingdoms and peoples and things!"

And even that man—*even Nebuchadnezzar*—
when he said, *"Please forgive me,"* God had the great pleasure—
in the wink of an eye, just as quick as a flash—
of tossing his sins out *for good* with the trash.

There's *never* been *anyone*. . .
There *never* will be—
who GOD can't forgive.
Try it. You'll see!

I HAVE A **STRANGE** TALE . . .

I have a strange tale I've been meaning to tell,
about a young fellow I know fairly well.
And so, if you've got a spare minute or two,
I'd be ever so happy to tell it to YOU!

How strange could it be? Oh, come on—you know ME.
It's as strange as a tale could impossibly be!

"Hey Pop," I exploded, "wake up and get dressed.
I've got a few things to get off of my chest!"

"I've had ALL I can stand. I can't stand any more!
This place is the pits. It's a snooze. It's a bore.
I'm a-gettin' on out while the gettin' is good,
and I'm not looking back till I reach Hollywood!

And oh yes, by the way—if you'd do me ONE favor,
it really *would* be a tremendous time-saver—
all that money you said that I'd get you-know-when,
well I want it RIGHT NOW! So go get it, amen?"

Well, to my great surprise, he forked over the loot.
And he did it without a bark, peep, or hoot.
So I packed up my bags and I ran for the hills.
I ran for the fun and the sun and the thrills!

I did my own thing. Man, I had it my way.
It was wall-to-wall, non-stop, just-do-it. Hooray!
It was wild. It was great. It was way-cool, far-out. . .

*Right on up to the point where the money ran out!*

Well, I got pretty hungry. I needed some food.
So I got me a job with a farmer-type dude,
who said, "I've got the thing for you here, Mr. Big—
you'll be feeding this awful green stuff to my pig."

"To your PIG?" I inquired. "That's why you were hired!
So do it right now," he up-heaved, "or you're fired!"
So, what's the big deal? Just go give him some chow?
Well that's easy for YOU to say, isn't it now!

This pig was no teeny, pink, pork-and-bean weenie.
THIS pig was a curly-tailed, wild-eyed *meanie*—
a big, bad, Tasmanian, pot-bellied sow—
a thousand-pound, honey-glazed ham-hock, and how!

So feed him I did—every night and each day.
I'd ker-plop that green glop and he'd chomp it away—
and I knew if I didn't eat something real soon,
I'd be in there MYSELF with a fork and a spoon.

My stomach was empty. My clothes were a mess.
"Oh, why did I do what I did?" I confessed.
I'm sure that my Father won't take me back now.
I *just* can't see why. No, I just can't see how!

I don't want my room or my robes or my rings.
No, I can't ask for ANY of those kinds of things.
I'M NO LONGER WORTHY OF BEING HIS SON!
Oh, why did I do it? Oh, why did I run!?

I'll ask for a job—just a job—nothing more.
I'll clean out the stable. I'll polish the floor.
I'll take out the trash—yes, I'll even do that.
I'll live out in back, on the porch, with the cat!

That ought to do it. Yes, that's what I'll say.
Then maybe he'll think about letting me stay.

So I packed up my bags and I ran from the hills.
But the thing I saw *next* really gave me the chills!

And the thing that I saw was that FATHER of mine. . .
He was waiting right there for me, all of the time!

"MY SON HAS COME HOME!" There were *tears* in his eyes!
Well, I have to admit, that was quite a surprise.

"Kill our best calf! Make a feast fit for kings!
Go and get my best robe—my best shoes—my best ring!
Everyone! Quickly! Come gather around!
Oh, my son who was lost, my dear SON, *he is found!*"

Well, I learned something then on that day, in that place.
Yes, I learned of my Father's great love and His grace.

And I learned that it's not what you do or you've done,
but I learned that it's *Jesus*—God's only Son—
who's the one and the ONLY one-way to be free. . .

He will take YOU back, too.
Go on—*ask Him!* You'll see!

# THE GOOD SAMARITAN

A WALK," I THOUGHT...

"A walk," I thought. "Now, that sounds nice—
like paradise to be precise.
To Jericho. Yes, that will be
the thing to do today for me!"

But, oh my word, I never knew.
I never even had a clue
my jog-for-joy would turn into
a rendezvous with *you-know-who!*

You don't know who? Oh, sure you do.
I'll bet your Grandma knows him, too!

I strolled along. I sniffed the breeze.
Aaah, chamomile and peonies!
Yes, columbine and hollyhocks—
sweet lavender and creeping phlox.

Oh bliss! Oh joy! Oh, hybrid teas,
all borne upon the balmy breeze,
with honeysuckle—strawberries—
magnolia trees and. . .

# STINKY CHEESE?

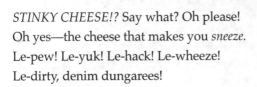

*STINKY CHEESE!?* Say what? Oh please!
Oh yes—the cheese that makes you *sneeze.*
Le-pew! Le-yuk! Le-hack! Le-wheeze!
Le-dirty, denim dungarees!

"Oh dear!" thought me. "What could it be?"
And then I spun around to see. . .

Two big, old, hairy, mean, and scary
guys who any momentary
planned to take my happy day
and turn it 'round the other way!

They shook me up. They knocked me down.
They hauled me halfway back to town.
They snitched my clothes and snatched my cash.
They pulled and twisted my mustache.

Oh, Grandma told me not to go
down on the road to Jericho!

I tried to move, but nothing budged.
I'd been completely chocolate-fudged.
I needed help, to say the least.

That's when I saw the temple priest!

"Oh, icky poo. Now what is THAT
untidy mess?" the high-priest spat.

"That's really gross. How impolite,
to lay there right where I just might
be forced to look at such a sight.
Oh great, there goes my appetite."

And then with that, he took his feet,
and crossed them right across the street.

You're right. I should have been upset.
But listen, it's not over yet. . .

I heard the sound of soulful singing.
Psalms and hymns and tambo ringing.
Harps and zithers. Bells and whistles.
Holy rock and rolled epistles!

Man, I love that gospel sound!
That sound's the best dressed sound around.
And this guy, *he* could play it right.
THIS guy was really out of sight.

I guess he didn't see me there.
That must be why he didn't care
to stop and say, "How do you do?"
I would have stopped. Well, wouldn't *you?*

Of course you would. Of course you should.
Of course I fully understood,
that if you could you surely would,
*but that won't do ME any good!*

Who's *THAT*, you say? Who's *who*? Who's where?
OH NO! NOT THAT GUY OVER THERE!

When THAT guy gets a hold of me,
I'll be as boo-booed as can be!
I tell you, there has NEVER been
a truly good Samaritan.

Oh yes, I know. I'm so ashamed!
I never, *ever* should have blamed
that precious, tender, gentle man—
that godly, good Samaritan.

He patched up all my lumps and thumps.
He *bandaged* all my boo-boo bumps.
He rode me back on into town,
then picked me up and set me down—

yes, set me down without a sound
right in the best hotel around!

This cannot be! Not HIM—not ME.
This man's as puzzling as can be.

But he was warm, and true, and real.
He told me Jesus Christ could *heal*
my busted, broken, banged-up heart. . .

So I said *yes,* it's time to start.

# The Pharisee and the Tax Collector

Luke 18:9–14

Two men went to church one day.
They went to church so they could pray.
Two men as different as can be—
the tax-man and the Pharisee.

The *Phari-who?* The Pharisee!
And who, pray tell, or what is he?
Well, if you listen carefully
I'm sure that soon you'll start to see!

The tax-man wasn't one to pray.
He never knew quite what to say.
His tongue got tangled up in knots—
it *would not* speak religious thoughts!

But when a *Pharisee* would pray,
he'd always pray the *proper* way. . .

"I thank You, God, as well I ought,"
he'd Phari-say, "that *I am NOT*

a lumpy, grumpy, slimy, sleazy,
smelly, dirty, grimy, greasy,
ooey-gooey, icky-pooey,
fellow through and through and through me!"

"I fast TWO whole times per week.
I'm helpful, friendly, kind, and meek.
But wait, there's more—oh yes, it's true—
I'm modest, pure, and humble, too!"

"Remember, I tithe ten percent
of every cent I ever spent.
Not ten-point-one, or nine-point-three,
but TEN percent—exact-o-ly!"

The Pharisees were quite content.
Their righteousness was evident.
But *tax collectors*, as you'll see,
were nothing like the *Pharisees*.

They taxed for this. They taxed for that.
They taxed you when you tipped your hat.
They taxed you when you blew your nose.
They taxed that stuff between your toes!

They said, *"That's just the way it goes. . ."*

*. . .then taxed your Grandma's underclothes!*

Now, every tax collector knows

he's *hated* everywhere he goes.

The tax collector never pled.
He never even raised his head.
"Oh God, have mercy. I have sinned."
Yes, that was all the old man said.

"What kind of goofy prayer is that?"
the Pharisee guffawed and spat.

"Oh God, as You can surely see,
THIS *tax-man* here is not like ME.
Yes, I could set THIS fellow straight.
But not right now. It's getting late—
*my Bible study starts at eight!*"

So off they went along their way.
And God forgave ONE man that day.
ONE MAN went home as white as snow.
But which one? Tell me, do you know?

Now, I *don't* think that God's impressed
by what we say, or how we dress—
or what we do, or did, or don't—
or what we will, or what we won't.

That's *outside* stuff. It's all okay.
It isn't wrong, unless one day
we find we're looking down our nose
and snorting, *"I'm not one of those!"*

For *"one of those"* needs one of YOU
to share the things that GOD can do!

# The parable of the vineyard workers

Matthew 20:1–16

*"The first shall be last and the last shall be first!"*

So, you think that the words must have gotten reversed?
Well, I'll tell you a secret: that's what I thought, too!
Oh, but not anymore—and soon *neither will YOU!*

A man had a vineyard. An honest, fair man.
And this honest, fair man really needed a hand...

"I'll give you all one whole denarius each,
if you're willing to work," he besought and beseeched,
"in my fields for the day, where you'll trudge and you'll traipse
back and forth, up and down, as you harvest my grapes."

Now, *one whole denarius,* that was some loot,
just for trudging and traipsing and picking up fruit.
"We've all hit the jackpot!" the workers yahoodled.
"To pass up THIS deal would be out-of-your noodled!"

So work they all did. Yes, they picked and they plucked.
They scooted and scampered and toted and trucked.
They gave thanks to the Lord for their awesome good-lucks,
for quite soon they'd be making the big, mega-bucks.

They worked very hard. Yes, they gave it their best.
They all huffed and they puffed without taking a rest.
But they couldn't keep up, so right back into town
went that honest, fair man to see who could be found
that would rather be working than standing around.

He went back there at nine, noon, and three on the dot.
Yes, he went back FOUR times—to the very same spot.
And every last time he'd just give the same speech:
*"One whole, bright, shiny denarius each!"*
and they'd run for his field just like kids at the beach.

Oh, and wouldn't you know, they got all the work done.
Yes the plucked every grape out there under the sun.
And that honest, fair man was as pleased as could be.
They had done what they said, and now, yes—*so would he!*

"What a beautiful, wonderful sight," thought the man.
"Every ONE worked *so hard*—now I think that we can
call it quits for the day, and with that I will say,
'It was fun. Thanks a ton. Come and pick up your pay.'"

"Call up the paymaster. Give them their dough.
Tell them all *thank you*, and then they can go.
Line them all up so the last ones are first,
and give them their one-tiny, bright-shiny, mine-finally
pure-silver coin so they're all reimbursed."

Now, one whole denarius, that was some loot,
just for trudging and traipsing and picking up fruit.
But the men who were hired way back at the first
were beginning to think that THEIR deal was *the worst!*

"Now listen here, mister, we started at *dawn!*
You're paying these *new guys* the same? Oh, come on!"
"We've been robbed!" they all shouted. "We huffed and we puffed,
and now what do we get? We get *not-near enoughed!*"

Well, that honest, fair man knew those men were upset.
But he gave every man what he said they would get.
So he opened his heart. He had something to say.
And the thing that *he said* really blew them away!

"I gave EACH OF YOU what I said you would get,
and *I know you worked hard,* but don't ever forget—
I NEVER said those who worked *more* were the best.
*I give all men the same.* No one more—no one LESS."

"God's love can't be earned. If it could, we would boast.
He loves all men the same. He loves no man the most!"

You can bop till you drop. That's okay, but it's true:
It will never depend upon how much you do.
When you come unto Him, *He will come unto you. . .*

That's a pretty good deal, I would say. Wouldn't you?

Fantastic. Amazing! They'll never believe it.
It's such a surprise, I can hardly conceive it.

An hour ago, I was locked in a cell
full of jeeper-creep-peepers and dust-musty smells.
I was chained to the wall. I was chained to the door.
I was chained to the lamp and the chair and the floor!

Then a voice, still and small, like a beautiful light,
whispered, "Peter, look up!" and to my great delight. . .

My chains were all broken. I was up on my feet.
I was out of that prison and back on the street!

Now, as you might have guessed, I was rather excited
to be so completely removed and uprighted.
I flew down the alley. I kicked up the dust.
I raced through the darkness, full-speed-ahead plus. . .

Finish the story? Get on with it? Do it?!
All right, just sit tight, and I'll get around TO it!

"Start at the start." That's what Mom used to say.
There was just no forgetting that one certain day. . .
We were washing our nets. We'd been fishing all night,
and my brother and I had a terrible fight.

"It's a beautiful fish, I would tend to agree,
and the only one singular fish that I see.
After thirty-one hours of huffing and sweating,
there's one teeny, tiny, small thing you're forgetting."

"One trivial, trifling, petty, slim thought. . ."

"IN A DAY AND A HALF,
THIS IS ALL
THAT WE'VE
CAUGHT!"

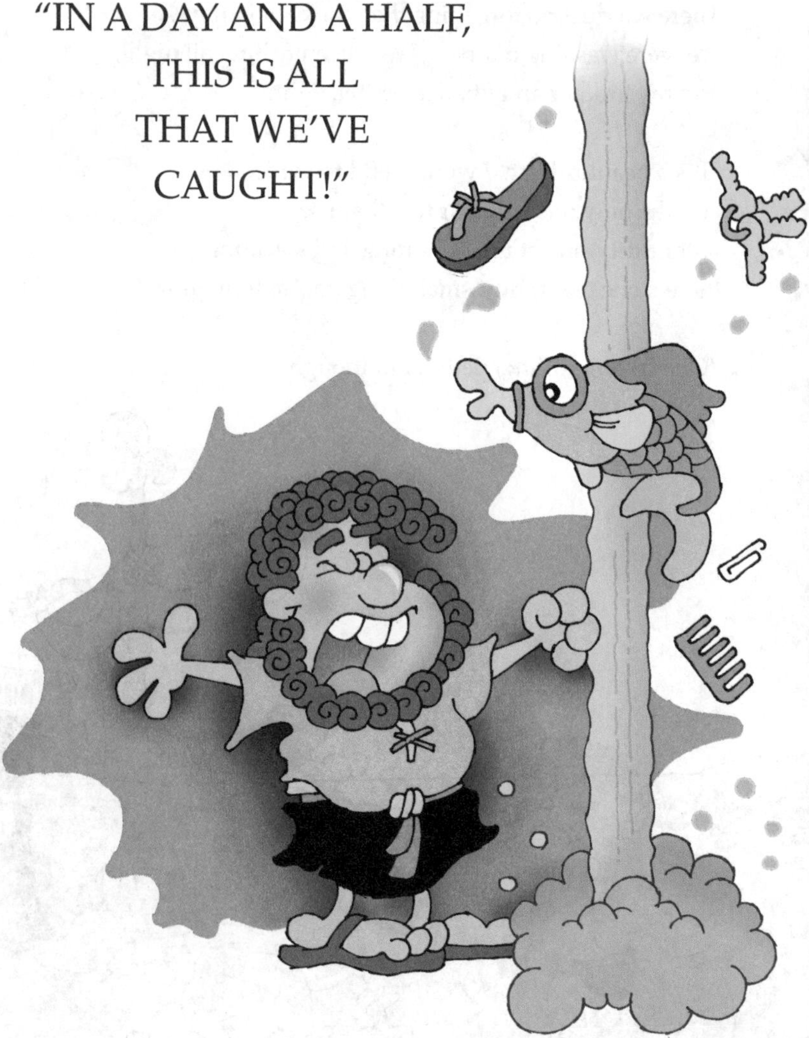

I was frothing and foaming, sautéing and stewing,
yes, gritting and grinding and chafing and chewing!

I was so caught away in my little black cloud
that I never did notice the wonderful crowd
of a hundred, or maybe a thousand or more,
who squash-squeezed and crunch-crowded their way to the shore.

"Teach us, O Lord!"
I heard them all shout
as they hustled
and bustled
and fussled about.

And there went my brother.
He was shouting it, too.
Why, the place had turned into
some kind of a zoo!

And, that's when it happened. He came up to me,
this man they were eyeing and trying to see.
He stepped into my boat, and He asked for a lift;
so I hoisted the sail, and I set her adrift.

"Cast out your nets," He proclaimed, "if you wish,
and you'll find that they're filled full to bursting with fish."

"Whatever you say. . ." This should really be good!
We'll probably snag a few pieces of wood,
or maybe some cans or a shoe or a boot
or a water-logged wallet. Now that would be cute!

But what happened next was a little bit shocking.
It sent my head spinning. It set my knees knocking!

Fish by the tens and the hundreds of dozens—
fish uncles and aunts, nephews, nieces, and cousins—
were cramming my nets. And before I could blink,
my poor boat was so full that it started to sink.

"Oh, Lord!" I cried out as I fell at His feet
and proceeded to whimper and sniffle and bleat.
"Go away from me, please. Oh, just leave me alone!
I'm the worst kind of horrible man ever known."

But HE didn't care. It was perfectly fine.
I could tell as His eyes looked down deep into mine.
And *right then and there,* in that boat, on that day,
Jesus wiped all my badness and sadness away.

235

But if *you* think *that's* something, then listen to *this*,
because this will be something you won't want to miss. . .

I remember that night, as the sun slowly set.
How we laughed! How we ate! Who could ever forget?
But while we were munching and chomping and chewing,
I noticed this strange thing that Jesus was doing.

He'd taken a bowl and a towel and a seat,
and proceeded to wash every one of our feet.
Our feet, of all things! Yes, He sat there among us.
He plucked every toe-jam and flushed every fungus!

"Not my feet, Lord! No, they itch and they scratch.
There just is no end to the things You might catch!
I'm certain there's something important to do,
for someone who's someone like someone like You. . ."

Well, He looked at that bowl, and I knew in a minute
He wanted my two big, fat feet to be in it!

"All right, then," I blubbered, "well, how about this. . ."

"I'll go get a sponge and a mop and a hose,
and we'll scrubble and bubble my knees and my nose.
Then we'll wish-wash my eyebrows and swish-swash my hips.
We'll polish my forehead and lather my lips!"

"Calm down. Pull the plug, Peter. Put it on ice!
Can't you see that I'm trying to do something nice?
Just relax," Jesus whispered, "and listen up well,
because now I'm the one with a story to tell!"

The story He told us was shocking and frightening.
Our eyes were bug-bulging, our stomachs twist-tightening.

He said He'd be battered, bruised, beaten, and killed;
but the Word of the Lord would at last be fulfilled!

Then, to top it all off,
He said I would deny
that I ever did know Him!
"Oh, no, Lord!" I cried.

"Before the cock crows, you'll deny Me three times."
How I wished I could get those words out of my mind.
As they dragged Him away, we were yelling and screaming.
This can't be for real. I just have to be dreaming!

"Hey, you with the beard and the big bony knees,
come on over here, we'd like to talk to you, please!
*We know* your face, and we know it *quite well.*
You were with Him, that Jesus. We know. We can tell!"

"Yes, I saw him, too. There can't be any doubt!"
an old, gravelly-gray, dusty voice gurgled out.
"I know you were there, you could hardly be missed."

*"You're mistaken!"* I bellowed and boiled and hissed.
"Mind your own business! Get out of my sight!

# I DON'T KNOW THE MAN—

*so just drop it, all right?"*

Yes, I denied Him, and they crucified Him.
I watched as they did it. I stood right beside Him.
But there's something I think that you really should know.
It's something He told me a long time ago. . .

"Peter," He said, "I AM LOVE, and you'll find
that I'm ever so patient and wonderfully kind.
I'm NOT keeping a list. I'm NOT checking it twice.
No, THAT would be naughty and not at all nice."

Oh, I've messed it up now. Lord, I've messed it up then.
Yes, I've messed it up over and over again.
Dear Lord Jesus, forgive me. Please bring me back home.
I'm the worst kind of horrible man ever known.

But the past is forgotten. Erased! Oh, it's true.

He did it for me. He WILL do it for you!

# Jesus and Nicodemus

John 3:1–21

Oh, not again. Just what we need—
a thousand porky piglets freed!
A mile-long sausage-link stampede,
hog wild and crazy guaranteed!

He must be here. He's back in town.
Yes, every time He comes around
this town just seems to come undone.
Just LOOK—here comes another one!

OH, NOT AGAIN!

That man was *lame!* How strange. How odd.
He's walking—leaping—praising God!
And over THERE! Oh, fear! Oh, dread!
Last week that guy right there was *dead!*

How can this BE? I have to see
this man from down in Galilee!
What's that? You want to see Him, too?
Okay. Let's go. I'll follow *you!*

Who am I? What do I do?
I'm Nicodemus. Who are you?
What's THAT? That's my phylactery.
You see, I am a *Pharisee.*

A Phari-WHO? A Pharisee!
And who, pray tell, or what is he?
Well, if you listen carefully,
I'm sure that soon, you'll start to see.

It started quite some time ago,
and I was there, so I should know!
I saw it all. The shame—*disgrace*—
at Matthew, the tax collector's, place. . .

That place? Oh dear! The scent. The smell!
And, *oh my word*—the clientele!
I've never seen a meaner bunch
all gathered up for Sunday brunch.

The house was packed with thugs and brutes
and folks with bad and ill-reputes.
Hoodlums! Gangsters! Outlaws! Cads!
Villains, rogues, and crooks—*EEEGADS!*

And there among the bums and brutes,
the rascals, thugs, and big-galoots,
sat *JESUS!* Eating—laughing—talking!
Loving! Teaching! Shameful! SHOCKING!

Dirty hands and dirty feet.
Dirty things to drink and eat!
Dirty hearts and dirty heads—
He didn't mind. He *loved* instead!

Now as you know, or may have guessed,
that left my heart a bit distressed.

And so, that night, without a peep,
once everyone had gone to sleep,
I slipped out on my hands and knees
and tiptoed through the tulip trees—

beneath the stars, there by the sea,
I met the man from Galilee!

I looked at Him. He looked at me.
His eyes were meek and *wild* and free.
It seemed to me like He could see
right through the hardest Pharisee!

He reached deep down inside my heart
and gently filled up every part.
I didn't know quite what to say,
but oh, it came out anyway.

"Jesus, please—before you go,
there's one small thing I have to know.

It's clear that you've been sent by God,
for *who* could doubt, the way You've awed,
amazed, astonished, and impressed us—
honored, cherished, loved, and blessed us!

Changed the water into wine—
healed the sick time after time—
raised men up from in the grave. . .
*But, what must I DO to be saved?"*

"Oh, *THAT'S* easy," Jesus said.
"No need to kneel or bow your head.
For God to live inside, My friend,"
He said, *"You must be born again!"*

"BORN again! BORN AGAIN?
How can a man be BORN again?
That will not work. That does not wash.
Not here, or in Oshkosh, b'gosh!

How can a man so big and smelly
get back in his mommy's belly?
Should I, could I, if I would?
*I WOULD NOT, even if I could!*

I would not sleep inside a crib,
or eat my breakfast with a bib,
or dribble oatmeal down my chin.
NO! I CAN NOT be born AGAIN!

Wear a pair of baby-booties?
Dress in lace and tootie-fruities?

Take my bath inside the sink,
all shriveled, wrinkled-up, and pink,
while everyone begins to shout,
'Let's go and get our cameras out!'

OH NO, I WON'T!
NOT ME. NO WAY—

*No matter what You do or say!*

I will not wear a big, fat Huggie,
ride inside a baby buggy,
rub-a-dub or splish and splash,
then get a case of diaper rash!

I can not do the thing you say.
The thing you say *is not okay!*
Not here. Not there. Not now. Not then.
No, I CAN NOT be BORN AGAIN!"

"Oh, Nicodemus," Jesus said,
"I don't mean born *like that* again.
Your outsides are just fine, My friend.
Your HEART—*that* must be born again.

For God so loved this world that He
gave up His only Son—*that's Me!*
and all who trust Me deep inside
will LIVE and never, ever die!"

*"I AM the Way. The Truth. The Life.
The First. The Last. Yes, Jesus Christ.*

*Behold, I stand—I stand and knock,
and wait for you to come unlock
the door that leads into your heart—
the door that's keeping us apart.*

*Please let me give MY life to you.
Oh, that is what I long to do!"*

So do I did. Well, wouldn't you?
Of course you would! You'd do it, too!
You'd let Him in right on the spot.
You'd say, "Okay! Of course! Why not!"

My soul was clean. My sins were crushed!
My stone-cold heart was corn-meal-mushed.
I once was blind, but now I see—
For Jesus lives *inside of me!*

This book is provided by

# **TRUTH**FOR**LIFE**

THE BIBLE-TEACHING MINISTRY OF **ALISTAIR BEGG**

At Truth For Life, our mission is to teach the Bible with clarity and relevance so that unbelievers will be converted, believers will be established, and local churches will be strengthened.

Since 1995, Truth For Life has aired a Bible-teaching broadcast on the radio, which is now distributed on over 1,600 radio outlets each day, and freely on podcast and on the Truth For Life mobile app. Additionally, a large content archive of full-length Bible-teaching sermons is available for free download at www.truthforlife.org.

Truth For Life also makes full-length Bible teaching available on CD and DVD. These materials, and also books authored by Alistair Begg, are made available at cost, with no markup, so that price is not a barrier to those seeking a deeper understanding of God's Word.

The ministry connects with listeners at live listener and pastor events and conferences across the U.S. and Canada in cities where the radio program is heard.

Contact Truth For Life

In the U.S.:

PO Box 398000, Cleveland, OH  44139 1.888.588.7884

www.truthforlife.org    letters@truthforlife.org

In Canada:

P.O. Box 19008, Delta, BC V4L 2P8   1.877.518.7884

www.truthforlife.ca    letters@truthforlife.ca

And also at:

www.facebook.com/truthforlife    www.twitter.com/truthforlife